MW01100673

GAS GIRLS

GAS GIRLS

DONNA-MICHELLE ST. BERNARD

PLAYWRIGHTS CANADA PRESS
TORONTO

PLAYWRIGHTS CANADA PRESS
The Canadian Drama Publisher
215 Spadina Ave., Suite 230, Toronto, ON, Canada M5T 2C7
phone 416.703.0013 fax 416.408.3402
info@playwrightscanada.com • www.playwrightscanada.com

For professional or amateur production rights, please contact
Angela Rebeiro, Kensington Literary Representation
34 St. Andrew St., Toronto, ON M5T 1K9
phone 416.979.0187, email kensingtonlit@rogers.com

Playwrights Canada Press acknowledges the financial support of the
Government of Canada through the Canada Book Fund and the Canada
Council for the Arts, and of the Province of Ontario through the Ontario
Arts Council and the Ontario Media Development Corporation, for our
publishing activities.

 Canada Council Conseil des Arts  ONTARIO ARTS COUNCIL
for the Arts du Canada CONSEIL DES ARTS DE L'ONTARIO

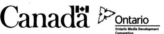

Cover photo © Keith Barker
Cover and type design by Blake Sproule

LIBRARY AND ARCHIVES CANADA CATALOGUING IN PUBLICATION
St. Bernard, Donna-Michelle
Gas girls / Donna-Michelle St. Bernard.

A play.
Issued also in electronic formats.
ISBN 978-0-88754-966-3

I. Title.

PS8637.A4525G37 2011   C812'.6   C2011-901203-0

First edition: August 2011
Printed and bound in Canada by AGMV Marquis, Montreal

To Brenda, an inspiring friend/fan/teacher/mom, and to my three favourite boyfriends.

CONTENTS

FOREWORD

When Donna-Michelle accepted her award for Outstanding New Play at the Doras, she told the audience that *Gas Girls* was part of "a 54-ology," a series of plays about Africa—one for each country. She got a huge laugh, but she wasn't kidding. Donna-Michelle's vision of the world includes Africa—all of Africa—as well as a number of other geographies including Toronto, paradise, and high school.

Gas Girls started, the story goes, after Donna-Michelle read about women along the Zimbabwe border who traded sex for gas. From that scant story were born Gigi and Lola, who trade

Love for gas
Gas for cash
Cash for living
Living for love.

One of the girls is fast, one is slow, and Gigi, the quick one, the clever girl, teaches Lola, the slow one, how to survive. The age of our heroines, mere teens, makes their situation that much more distressing. The play begins with a game of patty cake that evolves into a step dance, insisting the audience remember that these girls are just that: girls; girls barely out of childhood, girls who should be in school, who should be dreaming of the future.

From that moment of innocence and freedom the play carries us into the reality of their lives. Gigi, the elder at nineteen, serves as Lola's mother and madam, teaching her about condoms and the onset of her menses; about how to stay alive; whether, how, and where she services her clients; and how to prepare cassava. Gigi, at only nineteen, is also caring for her amai, who is bedridden and dying.

In spite of the grim circumstances, *Gas Girls* is hopeful; at times breathtakingly, achingly hopeful, allowing audiences a glimpse of redemption for at least one of the girls. The women love. They love each other, their families, their very lives. They dream too, telling each other stories of better places, better times, of *Sometime* when they go to school, marry, have children, and are loved. I have read many of Donna-Michelle's plays in many stages of development (not all, because she is preternaturally prolific), but the first time I read *Gas Girls* I was enchanted. The world of Gigi and Lola, of Chickn and Mr. Man, is so vivid and so compelling that I cared about the characters long after the last words on the last page.

As writers we are told to write about what we know. Donna-Michelle started writing the 54-ology before she ever set foot on African soil (though she has begun her pilgrimage now with trips to Mozambique, Uganda, and Kenya), but the continent is in her blood, and in her heart. Donna-Michelle has an overdeveloped sense of justice, but her plays are never didactic. Quite the opposite, they are often oblique beyond easy explanation. Her plays bloom miraculously on the journey from the page to the stage, which is what good theatre does. They are theatre pieces; they live fully in the voices of the characters, served by the voices of actors, those magicians of the theatre. And she *is* writing about what she knows, about injustice, about the hierarchy that leaves women with so little power. She knows what women will do to survive, to feed and shelter their families. She knows that "even love gonna kill you, you needen it too much."

Donna-Michelle knows about the cost to women, to mothers, to the great metaphorical mother, Earth, of the way we are living. It's in this way her Africa plays, indeed all of her plays, speak to us, whether we live in an urban Canadian centre or a dusty Zimbabwean border town; they demand we look at how we treat each other, how we care for each other, or don't care for each other, in the most dire of circumstances.

—Yvette Nolan, 2011

PLAYWRIGHT'S NOTE

Characters speak in a dialect unique to this play as opposed to one derived from a specific geography. Words ending in "en" indicates an elastic sense of word tense. For example, "You looken young" = "You look young" (present), "What you getten, these?" = "What are you going to get for these?" (future), "They given you something?" = "Did they give you something?" (past).

Gas Girls was first produced by New Harlem Productions at the Theatre Passe Muraille Backspace in November 2009, with the following cast and crew:

Peter Bailey: Mr Man (Henry)
Jamie Robinson: Chickn
Nawa Nicole Simon: Lola
Sodienye Waboso: Gigi

Director / dramaturge: Philip Adams
Set and costume designer: Jackie Chau
Lighting designer: Michelle Ramsay
Sound designer: Nick Murray
Stage manager: Stephanie Nakamura

Gas Girls was the recipient of the 2009 Enbridge playRites Emerging Playwright Award, the winner of the 2009 Herman Voaden Playwriting Award, named Outstanding New Play at the Dora Awards, and nominated for three other Doras, including Outstanding Male Actor for Jamie Robinson, Outstanding Female Actor for Nawa Nicole Simon, and Outstanding Set Design for Jackie Chau.

CHARACTERS

Gigi: nineteen-year-old highway girl, fast
Lola: fifteen-year-old highway girl, slow
Mr. Man: forty-five, transnational trucker who frequents the pit-stop market
Chickn: twenty-one, Lola's brother, Gigi's crush, a "merchant" at market

1. ADOLESCENCE

Music. GIGI and LOLA perform a patty cake that evolves into a step dance—innocence to survival. Turning what you know into a tool.

2. FU NOTHING PERSONAL

Truck stop. It's dusk, and traffic is heard passing by sporadically, mostly trucks and semis. Voices are heard from inside the truck parked to one side of the highway.

MR. MAN clears his throat once, and then again, prolonged. A pause.

GIGI   Is that what you wanted?

MR. MAN   Yes.

GIGI   We call it sou-sou.

MR. MAN	Mm.
GIGI	Tell me what you callen it again?
MR. MAN	Tollie-lekke.
GIGI	Tollie-lekke. Too long.
MR. MAN	I hear that a lot.
GIGI	Very funny.
MR. MAN	It is a terrible burden.
GIGI	Only for me.
MR. MAN	Not so terrible, eh?
GIGI	No. Not so.
MR. MAN	So… *(angling for another go round)*
GIGI	Okay, I gotta go.
MR. MAN	Aw c'mon, honey. One more time. Two for one. It's my birthday this year.
GIGI	No. I told you. Gotta get back to work.
MR. MAN	All right.
GIGI	So…
MR. MAN	Where's the can?
GIGI	Behind you. *(pissing/pouring sound)*

MR. MAN	Hand me my belt, honey.
GIGI	Okay. How far you goen today?
MR. MAN	Always the same question.
GIGI	Always wonder. If you were here you'd wonder too.
MR. MAN	Well, I'll tell you. Today I'm going eight hundred miles. Do you know where that will take me?
GIGI	Not here.
MR. MAN	Exactly.
GIGI	Exactly.
MR. MAN	You want a ride somewhere?
GIGI	Don't need it. Goen close.
MR. MAN	All right, what you still here for?
GIGI	Goen. *(backs into the street, truck departs, LOLA enters)*
LOLA	Gigi! Gigi! *(GIGI keeps walking.)* Gigi! You gonna wait for me?
GIGI	I gotta go, Lola.
LOLA	Looken like you in a hurry.
GIGI	Very good, Lola.
LOLA	Looken like you got no time for stopping.

GIGI	Smart today, huh?
LOLA	I like walking with you, only your legs too many times more long than mine. You walken with me, taken you twice as long.
GIGI	Yup.
LOLA	Time I get there, you already been twice.
GIGI	Okay, bye.
LOLA	Wait.
GIGI	—
LOLA	Do you have any condoms, Gigi?
GIGI	No, I use the last one. Chickn have some down the road.
LOLA	Dem well expensive down the road, Gigi.
GIGI	Dem the same expensive for me as they is for you.
LOLA	But look how you full up, girl.
GIGI	Must be I worked for this, not chasing somebody up the road.
LOLA	Not chasing. Keeping you company.
GIGI	You full up already?
LOLA	Yes.

GIGI	*(checks)* No. Can't have time for keeping company, then.
LOLA	Maybe I gonna go this way anyhow.
GIGI	Oh yeah? Where to, the mission?
LOLA	…
GIGI	Lola, you gone to the church?
LOLA	No.

GIGI *stifles laughter.*

You told me.

GIGI	They given you something?
LOLA	You was wrong. Dem church never give condoms. Only given me tea and one big talking. Dem talken too long, taken my whole day. My brother gets mad, I cheating him business. Chickn say my time is him money. Not a good idea, Gigi. *(rubbing her arm)* Maken Chickn so mad. Him say only Chucky come back swingen arms.
GIGI	Good. You need to learn, Lola. Gotta be thinken for yourself.
LOLA	You know is hard, G.
GIGI	Is de same hard for alla we, Lola.
LOLA	One day I gon cross de border and gone.

GIGI	One day, hein?
LOLA	Yeah, maybe. Chickn say tell you to come by... You have any saran?

GIGI hands her a small square, starts to leave, turns, and hands her a small bottle of mouthwash.

GIGI	Lola. You wash out your mouth after, hear?
LOLA	Okay, Gigi. *(exits)*
GIGI	And stop eaten dem dirt. *(lingers, sees a tire by the roadside, takes it with her)* Dis one nice and high.

Love for gas
Gas for cash
Cash for living
Living for love.

3. DOWN THE ROAD

GIGI's house. She and CHICKN outside the door.

CHICKN	Gigi, wanna come out?
GIGI	Out where?
CHICKN	Walk down the road some.
GIGI	Hm. What they got down the road?
CHICKN	Nothing.

GIGI	Got my own nothing here, Chickn. Why don't you come in? Enough nothing to share with you.
CHICKN	Come on, Gigi. We gonna go walk and talk a bit.
GIGI	Just talken?
CHICKN	Of course.
GIGI	Got talken here, too. Come in.
CHICKN	Okay, Gigi. Not just talken. Want to show you something down there.
GIGI	Chickn, I can't go.
CHICKN	Not far, not for long. Just down the road and back again.
GIGI	Chickn… sing me that song.
CHICKN	I'll sing it for you, all the way there and back again.
GIGI	Sing it for me now.
CHICKN	Then you'll come?
GIGI	Maybe.
CHICKN	Know this man can't be hungry When him fill up with your smile Know this man cannot be alone Because he is somebody's child.
GIGI	That's nice.

CHICKN	Come on. Let's go now.
GIGI	What you got there, down the road?
CHICKN	Can't tell it, Gigi. Gotta show you.
GIGI	Okay, tell me how far we'll go.
CHICKN	Not far.
GIGI	Is it... as far as the truck stop?
CHICKN	No, closer than that.
GIGI	Is it as far as Spitty's house?
CHICKN	Closer. You know that tree shape like bad luck, way down the road next to the church?
GIGI	Yeah.
CHICKN	Well, you know that tall rock that juts out around the corner?
GIGI	Yeah.
CHICKN	And you know, when you standen on that rock and looken way down the hill across the pitch, if you small up your eyes you can just see the top of the chimney on that brick shed?
GIGI	Yeah.
CHICKN	Well, it's much closer than that.

GIGI	Is it far as the hideaway place behind the market you showed Mimi last Wednesday? Or is it exactly as far as that?
CHICKN	Gigi, Mimi and me only doen business…
GIGI	Did she like your song, Chickn?
CHICKN	I never sing for Mimi.
GIGI	Well, I think I already seen what you showed her. I'm not coming out today. Maybe another time.
CHICKN	Which other time, Gigi? You think everybody's Lola?

4. BUSINESS NEVER PERSONAL

> *GIGI's house. Arriving home, GIGI leans the tire against the wall and puts the can in an elaborate hiding place under the bed with two other cans. She rests briefly, then takes out another elaborately concealed package from across the room. She unwraps it and counts coins.*

GIGI   Amai, my amai. Never mind tires. Tires just for now. Getten you a proper bed, soon. Good, soft bed gonna let you turn your body without twisten your face. Gotten enough to get dem medicine today, gonna hold you two weeks. Gotten just enough… Shit.

> *Calculates. She pulls a can from under the bed and reluctantly pours half of it into a smaller container,*

which she takes with her. She goes to market and passes
CHICKN as if she intends to keep going.

CHICKN   Gigi, you come here. What you got?

GIGI   How much you go gimme, dis?

CHICKN   *(whips out a bill and proffers it)* Ten. *(The note hangs be-*
              tween them.)

GIGI   Robbery, dat.

CHICKN   Is true, but is you robbing me.

GIGI   How so?

CHICKN   You want ten.

GIGI   Yes.

CHICKN   Same can cost me half dat on the open market.

GIGI   Really? Open market good to you. Why you wasten
              time with me?

CHICKN   Open market playen hard to get right now.

GIGI   You mean she run away. No gas, no soap, no milk.
              Nobody seen open market in a long time. You know
              something we don't?

CHICKN   Oh, I know where to find she.

GIGI   Really.

CHICKN	Yes, man! I just have to climb up de president leg and go look in him pocket.
GIGI	Oho! You ever see anybody go in de president pocket and come out again? You brave.
CHICKN	Not brave, smart. Him pocket fill up with so many police and judges. Only have to throw in a dollar and let them kill each other to get it while I shop.
GIGI	Sound like a lot 'a work. Better you stay here and give me twelve, dis.
CHICKN	Can not, Gigi. Can't break me for you. Can not.
GIGI	Why? You don't like me anymore?
CHICKN	Liken you all I want, ain't getten me nowhere. When you gonna come visit me at my house?
GIGI	And I'm doen what, at your house? Maybe some-time you ask me when I'm gonna stay. Not looken for places to visit, Chickn.
CHICKN	Just wanten to take care of you, Gigi.
GIGI	You wanten something, gonna learn to wait for it.
CHICKN	Good cassava don't good forever. Be careful you don't keep it till nobody want it.
GIGI	Good cassava don't pick before she ripe.
CHICKN	Okay, little more, Gigi.

He adds a bill and she accepts. Their hands and eyes touch and hold over the money.

Only you look out for Lola, yeah?

GIGI   Yeah. Your mama know where Lola at?

CHICKN   Walk down the road, she find out, eh?

GIGI   Chickn…

She's shy. He is too, then lets go of GIGI's *hand, seeing someone.*

CHICKN   …You stopping this way, Mimi? *(throws a rock at her)* Chucky you. Go on. Come here, Lola. Stay away from her and her ways.

LOLA runs over to GIGI.

GIGI   Bye, Chickn. *(walks a bit and hollers at another merchant)* Lemon Man! You gonna cut me a deal, dem dry-up lemons?

LOLA   *(picking at her foot)* Hi, Gigi.

GIGI   What's wrong with you?

LOLA   Nothing.

GIGI   You been worken?

LOLA   Yes.

GIGI   Outside?

LOLA	…No.
GIGI	Mm hm. So dis mud on your back from inside the truck.
LOLA	Yes.
GIGI	Not from behind dem bushes.
LOLA	No.
GIGI	Cuz I know you don't layen down in dem bush to do your business with dem ancients watchen you. Bad juju, dat.
LOLA	No, I didn't. And anyways, I didn't let them taste my life. Cuz you told me, Gigi. Once dem taste it dem want it all.
GIGI	Good. So I know you don't need any help getten them chiggers out your foot, because you can't getten no chigs burrowen in your foot, deep under the skin, maken you itch till you can't stand it, if you goen in the truck, right? Ain't lyen on the ground, can't get no eggs lay up under your skin, diggen deeper and deeper, up next to the bone where you scratch it till it bleed and still can't come near that itch. Not if you goen in the truck like a good girl. Right?
LOLA	Right.
GIGI	Cuz you know. Chucky get dirt, then—
LOLA / GIGI	Chucky get dead.
GIGI	Right?

LOLA	Right.

GIGI	Okay. Goodbye then.

> *GIGI exits slowly. LOLA tries to control the itching until GIGI is out of sight.*

LOLA	Chickn!

5. CHATBOUT

> *Truck stop. LOLA on all fours, MR. MAN zipping up, flipping her skirt back down. LOLA is transfixed by a shaft of light and does not get up.*

MR. MAN	Good to move my back after all that driving. *(stretches)* Get that little pull on the left side and nothing but road and more road to take your mind off it. Gotta work, gotta drive, right? Is what I'm gonna do instead? ...You hurt?

LOLA	No.

MR. MAN	You stuck?

LOLA	No.

MR. MAN	Come on, then. Up. I'm done here.

LOLA	Gotten one just like that at my house.

MR. MAN	Eh?

LOLA	Got one piece of light like that, my house. All dancen, comen down like that. Know how many pieces he got in that light? Too many. Even Chickn can't count all dem. Too many, and you try taken em in your hand, dem never leave that place. Known what they got inside them piece of light? Everywhere. Right there. All of it.
MR. MAN	That so?
LOLA	Sorry. Please don't— Sorry, all dem nonsense. I'm goen now.
MR. MAN	Now, hold on—
LOLA	Sorry. Sorry...

LOLA leaves. MR. MAN finds a ribbon from her hair in his truck.

MR. MAN	Pieces of light. Dem girls crazy. Remember this one driver, him always broke. Never carry more gas than he need to get there and back, down to the drop. Keepen him money for something, but nobody ever known what because him have no extra, so him never stop. Just driven to the base, turn around, driven back; eaten him money, I guess. But one time, he seen this girl. Never stop before and nobody know why this one girl catch him, but he seen this girl and he stop. Do him business. Drive on. Halfway back, him stranded beside the road, tank dry. And him stand there a long time, because a man who never have a thing spare can't be asken favours when him run dry. After a long wait him walk all the way to the next

truck stop, spend him little money and beg a can to carry him gas, walken all the way back to that truck. Now him have gas, but while he gone all dem tires get took. So tank full, but him still walken, knowen that gas gonna be gone by the time him get back with any tire. Nobody seen him again. That man ruined. Dem girls crazy.

6. BUTTERFLY DEFENCE

·   *Truck stop.*

CHICKN   Gigi! Gigi! Come take this foolish girl.

GIGI   What's goen on?

CHICKN   Come take her. Can't do business, this one hangen off me like a broken arm.

GIGI   Lola. Leave the man. Come, na. Chickn, what happen to her?

CHICKN   Nothing happen.

GIGI   Look like something.

CHICKN   Is nothing.

GIGI   Then I can't help, Chickn. Don't know how to fix nothing.

CHICKN   …Lola seen Spitty gun. She 'fraid to leave me. Somebody tell her to 'fraid guns. Somebody need to take her from me.

GIGI	Spitty got a gun now?
CHICKN	Is nothing. Somebody cheat him and him take a bag of yam to the base to trade for one rusty old pistol.
GIGI	Spitty can't piss straight. How him gonna shoot anybody?
CHICKN	Man with a gun never need to shoot. That man who cheat Spitty, him playing cards down the beach yesterday. When him feel that cold little circle on him neck, argument done.
GIGI	Done till that man come back again with more gun.
CHICKN	I hope not. Spitty don't have enough yam to buy bullets.
GIGI	Argument don't done like that.
CHICKN	What you know?
GIGI	I know better than to get mix up in bad business.
CHICKN	Is not everybody looken for it, Gi. Sometimes bad business find you.
GIGI	Maybe you. Lola. Lola, come here. Lola, Chickn goen to Spitty's house now. You wanna go with him?

LOLA shakes her head.

Come, then. Where your ribbon gone? Come let me braid your hair again.

7. UP THE ROAD

CHICKN's stand. End of the day. Vendors are dwindling away. Others try for day's-end bargains.

GIGI   Hey, Chickn.

CHICKN   *(packing up, stops)* What you need, Gigi? I'm just done.

GIGI   Don't need nothing. Just wanted to show you something.

CHICKN   Oh yeah?

GIGI   Yeah.

CHICKN   Mm. I don't know. How far is it?

GIGI   *(moving closer)* Very close.

CHICKN   Okay... let's go.

GIGI   Close your eyes.

CHICKN   *(flirting)* Make me.

GIGI   *(getting her space back)* Fine, don't. Don't matter.

CHICKN   Aw, Gigi.

GIGI   Okay, come on. *(He follows her to an abandoned truck.)* Here it is. *(presents truck)*

CHICKN   Where here, under dis junky?

GIGI	No junky, dis.
CHICKN	Really? Full up with gas, engine running good. Somebody just get tired riden and decide to leave she here, eh? Yes, then nobody find it till you find it. Good kinda lucky, you. Good car, dis. Tire only looken flat, is just sleepy. Door only looken rusty, is really blushing because you so pretty. No junky, dis. Go on, take me riden.
GIGI	I'm gonna.
CHICKN	*(laughing, gets in driver's seat)* Okay, get in. Where we goen?
	She indicates him over to passenger's side and sits in the driver's seat.
GIGI	*(pointing)* That way. *(starts the truck)*
CHICKN	You know something about driven this?
GIGI	This? Got an idea.
CHICKN	Been in plenty cars before, yeah?
GIGI	Trucks. *(beat)*
CHICKN	Okay. Let's go.
	GIGI drives down the road. CHICKN plays along.
GIGI	Here come Oba sneaker store. Dis corner tight. Hi, Spitty! Oops. Seen his shoeshine box go flyen? Look back for me. He looken mad to you?

CHICKN	*(looking behind them at Spitty)* Not very. He laughen too hard, to see you driven.
GIGI	Hm. Funny dat, eh? Maybe I'm gonna go back and try that corner again, faster. Maken Spitty real mad this time—gonna stop his laughen good. Maybe we go around again I'm gonna get the joke too.
CHICKN	Oh, looken like he done laughen. Go on. Forget Spitty.
GIGI	I forgotten him already.
CHICKN	Straight on, then.
GIGI	Ah, here we are.
CHICKN	We here?
GIGI	Yeah.
CHICKN	Getten out now?
GIGI	No, not yet. Now we looken.
CHICKN	Looken where?
GIGI	That way.
CHICKN	Okay. *(They look.)* What we looken at?
GIGI	*(pause)* Border. *(breathes)*
CHICKN	*(wrenching wheel)* Let's go back.

There is a tension between them as they drive back to where they started, awkwardly sitting for a moment after parking.

GIGI I better go home.

CHICKN You gonna walk with me a little way?

GIGI A little way.

LOLA *(showing up)* Been looken for you. Can I go home?

CHICKN You know the way, Lola?

LOLA Yes.

CHICKN You done worken?

LOLA Yes.

CHICKN Then you can go.

LOLA Where you goen?

CHICKN Nowhere.

LOLA Where you been?

GIGI Nowhere.

CHICKN Gigi been all over.

LOLA Oh, yeah. I been right over there. Looken for you. Let's go, Chickn.

GIGI	I better go home.
LOLA	Chickn.
CHICKN	You better.

8. SHIFTED

Truck stop. GIGI and MR. MAN negotiate.

GIGI	*(hopping back and forth from foot to foot)* All the way, then all the way full. Yeah?
MR. MAN	You looken young. Gonna cry on me?
GIGI	Only looken young. I been done this lots of times.
MR. MAN	Maybe too many times. Maybe you gonna be maken me sick.
GIGI	No, no. I been liven long enough, been clean always.
MR. MAN	Guess you think I gonna pay that condom.
GIGI	You give me a can, Mr. Man, we paid up.
MR. MAN	Turn around. *(GIGI does.)* Hmm. Where your brother is?
GIGI	Got none. Father either. I'm only me.
MR. MAN	Maybe you're lonely. Maybe you need friends more than business.

He opens both hands to grope her. She thrusts the gas can between his hands.

GIGI   All the way, then all the way full. Yeah?

MR. MAN   How much you getting on the other end, for one full can?

GIGI   All these questions. You maken me a bank manager?

MR. MAN   *(giving her an up-down appraisal)* Yeah, okay. Let's go.

GIGI   Shit. Wait. Gotta go pee first. *(goes, LOLA enters)*

LOLA   Gigi? Hey Gigi? *(seeing MR. MAN)* Oh, hi.

MR. MAN   Hello. How you?

LOLA   Good. Where Gigi go?

MR. MAN   Who? She gone away now. What you need?

LOLA   Done good. Only need half a can more.

MR. MAN   Then what?

LOLA   Then I get to go home.

MR. MAN   Me too.

LOLA   You too?

MR. MAN   Oh yeah. Only half a can to trade, then I can go home too. Only needen someone to take this one little half can before I can go all the way back home again to see my *ghoso*. Real lonely on that road.

LOLA	Must be you missen home, been driven so long. Must be you want to go home more than I do.
MR. MAN	Definitely.
LOLA	Looken like we got the same troubles.
MR. MAN	Maybe we help each other, hm?
LOLA	Hm?
MR. MAN	Lemme see. *(looks at her can)* Hm. Half already. That's good. All the way full, then all the way, yeah?
LOLA	*(thinks)* Yeah.
MR. MAN	Come on.

He leads her to his truck. She looks around at MR. MAN's stuff.

LOLA	Like a turtle, dis.
MR. MAN	Only need this small place to put your back. What you need more space for?
LOLA	On your back, like a turtle. Wishen I could take mine with me, too.
MR. MAN	Eh?
LOLA	Lucky, you. People like me got too much. Never gonna get away, you gotten too much stuff to carry. Lucky, you.
MR. MAN	Lucky me. *(They get down to it.)*

GIGI   *(returning)* Mr. Man? Damn. Better he don't pee. He
            finish faster he gotta go bad… Come on. Come on.
            (LOLA and MR. MAN return shortly.)

LOLA   How far you goen now?

GIGI   Lola!

LOLA   Hey, Gigi!

GIGI   Lola, I was going with Mr. Man. He gonna give me
            a whole can.

LOLA   But Gigi, he say he only wanna give half.

            MR. MAN laughs low and exits.

GIGI   Lola—

LOLA   It's okay, Gigi. He looken mad before. Mr. Man looken
            happy now, see? Remember you told me, we gonna
            make them happy.

GIGI   Lola… *(doesn't hit her)* Let's go, Lola. *(They walk.)*

LOLA   Gigi, tell me about Sometime.

GIGI   Not now.

LOLA   When?

GIGI   Later.

LOLA   Tell me about Sometime now.

GIGI	Sometime we gonna go back to school. Sometime I gonna make nice dresses all the ladies. You gonna make cassava cake. We gonna have market stall, husband gonna love us, kids be strong. Sometime they gonna go to school too. You gonna be smart, getten your hair straight, gonna come to the market in a car. *(a plane flies by overhead, both girls watch it)* Sometime you gonna ride the plane.
LOLA	Yeah. When Sometime coming?
GIGI	Never.
LOLA	*(They walk a bit.)* Gigi... when Never coming?
GIGI	Never mind. Lola, nobody know when Sometime comes. One day it's just gonna get here, and you got no time for thinken. Just gotta go.
LOLA	You gonna come get me?
GIGI	For what?
LOLA	If Sometime comes, you're not gonna leave without me.
GIGI	Sure, Lola. I'll come get you.
	LOLA tries to lean her head on GIGI's shoulder. GIGI shakes her off.
LOLA	*(after a while)* Henry given me chocolate.
GIGI	Henry who?
LOLA	My friend, Henry, in the red truck, gotten two yellow birds painted on the door.

GIGI   Mr. Man's not your friend, Lola. Got no reason for
            needen his name.

LOLA   —

GIGI   No reason for talken to Mr. Man. Only tellen him
            how much and letten him do him business. I told
            you and told you. Him don't wanna hear you talken
            all dem nonsense in your head. Him don't care about
            you. Maken him mad, Mr. Man gonna put you under
            the tree. Shut you up. Share.

            *LOLA does and GIGI allows her to lay her head in her
            lap. They eat the chocolate.*

LOLA   Look what else Henry give me. *(opens and flicks a light-
            er)* We should find a cigarette.

GIGI   Gimme that. Lola, you got gas on your clothes?

LOLA   Just a little.

GIGI   You not allowed to hold a lighter. Got it? *(schupzes,
            pocketing lighter)* And wash that gas off your clothes
            tonight before Chickn smell it. Remember what he
            told you?

LOLA   Every drop spill today is bread off my plate tomorrow.

GIGI   Right. Okay, how much you got?

LOLA   *(taking coins from pocket)* Twenty-five.

GIGI   Go down there and get us some crackers.

LOLA   Gonna have nothing left.

GIGI	Better to be alive with light pockets, or hungry, heavy, and dead?
LOLA	Alive.

LOLA exits. GIGI takes out her own chocolate bar and eats it hoardingly. LOLA returns and sees her. GIGI puts the last piece in her mouth and extends a palm for crackers, which LOLA shares.

GIGI	Can't be taken my man, Lola.
LOLA	Didn't know.
GIGI	You know anything?
LOLA	No.
GIGI	Start again, then. *(This is accompanied by a handclap routine each time, a sequence taken from the opening.)* No kissing. No cutting. No freebies. No cuddling up.
LOLA	No kissing. No cutting. No freebies. No cuddling up. Gigi, I like cuddling up.
GIGI	You doing what you like, or you working?
LOLA	Working.
GIGI	Cuddling up gonna make you some money?
LOLA	No.
GIGI	If it's not maken your money, can't be taken your time. You go with Mr. Man for working, Lola. Chucky go for liken it. Chucky you?

LOLA	No.
GIGI	Good. No kissing. No cutting. No freebies. No cuddling up. No taken my man.
LOLA	No kissing. No cutting. No freebies. No cuddling up. No taken my man.
GIGI	Right. And next time you put your finger in your nose, gonna have Chickn cut it off for you.

LOLA puts her hand in her pocket.

Go away.

LOLA	Okay. *(does)*
GIGI	Love for gas Gas for cash Cash for living Living for love.

9. NOT TODAY

Truck stop. Inside MR. MAN's truck. GIGI touching up MR. MAN's belongings.

MR. MAN	Over here.
GIGI	What's this?
MR. MAN	Don't go back there. Just here is far enough.
GIGI	Calm down. Just wanten to see.

MR. MAN	Don't open that.
GIGI	Cool your heat, Mr. Man.
MR. MAN	My name's—
GIGI	Uh huh.
MR. MAN	What's your name?
GIGI	Who cares.
MR. MAN	Got this hairbrush for you. But I don't give gifts to strangers.
GIGI	…
MR. MAN	How'd you like it if I come in your house, touching all your things?
GIGI	Dis all the house you got?
MR. MAN	This mine.
GIGI	Dis plenty. Plenty dis.
MR. MAN	I don't think so. Pretty girl like you deserve more space. *(strokes her, then pushes her roughly)* So go. All the road yours now.

> GIGI *goes home and counts the money under the bed, then counts again. There is not much.*

GIGI	Shit.

GIGI takes out two cans of gas and goes to the market.
CHICKN is counting money, putting it away.

CHICKN   Yeah.

GIGI   Hey, Chickn.

CHICKN   Yeah.

GIGI   How's today?

CHICKN   Only sellen today, Gigi. Can't buy what you got.

GIGI   But I got—

CHICKN   *(preoccupied with a calculation)* Don't need it right now.
          See me tomorrow.

GIGI   Can't help me tomorrow. I need some now.

CHICKN   Can't help you now.

GIGI   What you getten these? Forty?

CHICKN   —

GIGI   Fifty!

CHICKN   Yeah.

GIGI   Gimme twenty these. Gimme twenty-one of these,
          I'll bring the rest tomorrow.

CHICKN   See me tomorrow, Gigi.

GIGI	Tomorrow can't help me. Chickn. Chickn. Chickn.
CHICKN	Doen business. Not doen helping. Got the mission for that. Gigi, you known how this works. If I go buyen what I don't need, I be out of business in a week. No business, no reason to stay. What you gonna do if I'm gone from here? Gonna sell your gas to Lemon Man?
GIGI	Chickn.
CHICKN	Tomorrow.
GIGI	Is only you could have money when you want it?
CHICKN	What I have? Huh? You go down there and tell Mimi I can have my money whenever I want it. You tell her gimme what she owes me; what she don't have. You think I have it any better than you? Pecken and scratchen in the dirt all day for one damned kernel of corn? It's every one of us hustling the same hustle, Gigi. You don't have it special hard.

GIGI walks back to her house.

10. SUN AND SEA

GIGI's house. GIGI is in her room, sitting on the bed, nursing a withered figure.

GIGI	Sometime you gonna come out of bed. Sometime I gonna make babies for you to see and teach your stories. Sometime we gonna fish that river. Fish gonna come back. *(opens a bottle)* You gonna drink this water, yeah? Gonna wash all the dust, your throat, feel

good and clean. Sometime, we gonna have trees, like before. Remember? Gonna push their roots under, so far, turn up all the earth, shaken dem little things live down there. Tree got a nice few years, gonna put down yams, keep dem roots company. Everything liven need some company, yeah? Nice fat yam, breaken open and the sun come out of dem. Never mind tired. Gonna be jumping over the fence when you come from the market, Sometime.

CHICKN   *(whispering from the door)* Gigi. *(rooster crows)* Gigi.

GIGI   *(coming to the door)* Yeah?

CHICKN   We going down to the beach. Spitty got a jug of palm.

GIGI   Can not, Chickn. Been gone too long already yesterday. Gotta stay here in case… anything.

CHICKN   Gonna leave early, be there by daybreak, back again before the bells. Come on, girl. Gonna be a good time. How many good times you haven, stayen here?

GIGI   What you mean? Always haven a good time here. Don't you know? Haven so many jokes with the roaches, rats get mad for the laughing.

CHICKN   Dem rats ain't bring palm wine, do they?

GIGI   No.

CHICKN   Dem smile at you like this? Dem sing. *(He sings.)* Come with me, baby.

GIGI   Think you're coming back early? I seen that jug of palm talk to make you slow. Talk loud enough, that jug of palm start to think for you. Thinken of trouble to get for you. Could be she talk too sweet one day, you never come back. Gone somewhere easy. Gone to the ocean, maybe.

CHICKN   Somebody should put another sweet talk in my ear, maybe I won't hear dem palm-wine whispers.

GIGI   Somebody like who?

CHICKN   Is only you I listenen for.

GIGI   Maybe another time.

CHICKN   Maybe another time. So, since you staying here today anyways…

GIGI   No. I don't wanna keep Lola today.

CHICKN   Lola tired. She don't wanna go so far, so early.

GIGI   And what else?

CHICKN   You know. Taken Lola, I can't do nothing. Gonna watch Lola all day from dem palm wine and dem town boys.

GIGI   Dem boys gonna leave Lola alone. Anyhow, she knows better.

CHICKN   Dem boys been looken at her enough in town. What's gonna happen, I bring her to the beach? Dem know what kind of girls dem have at the beach.

GIGI   What kind of girls dem have at that beach you gonna take me to?

CHICKN	Lola don't know better. Gonna make me nervous. Can't do nothing all day.
GIGI	And what you planning to do?
CHICKN	Nothing.
GIGI	So. No problem, then.
CHICKN	Gigi, pretty Gigi. *(tries to touch her)*
GIGI	Thought you weren't gonna stay all day, anyhow. Come here, Chickn.

> *She draws him into the house and uncovers a small stack of tires.*

Help me.

CHICKN	*(inspects them)* Blown out, all. Can't be sellen these.
GIGI	Not help sellen, help liften.

> *She drags the last tire into place and they lift the mattress onto the tire bed.*

There. Them chigs never jumpen this high.

> *GIGI removes the window covering and a shaft of light falls on the bed.*

(to her amai) Sun gonna shine your face. *(to CHICKN)* Okay. Tell Lola come by here. She gonna help me.

CHICKN	Thanks, Gigi. Another time, right?

GIGI	Sure, Chickn. Another time.
CHICKN	*(exiting)* Lola, come here.
LOLA	*(enters house)* We going to the beach, Gigi?
GIGI	You been good?
LOLA	Yes.
GIGI	Then Sometime we gonna go.

> GIGI *takes out a crumpled piece of newspaper and holds it up before her.* GIGI *points and* LOLA *sits in a corner as* GIGI *"reads" a story, soon giving up the reading pose for storytelling.*

The trees dem was bending in the wind off the ocean. Lola, gonna help me tell it?

> LOLA *makes the sound of wind and, successively, the ocean, a bird, etc.*

The trees dem was bending in the wind off the ocean. Nearly double, bending, looking for something dem lost on the ground, but that thing dem lost already rolled away. The sand be looking up at the waves comen over it, watching the washing. Seeing the sea. Sand be looken around and right up from her sandy little eye come a crab, diggen himself up, and bury himself down again. The sun, he look down and think he see the sand she winken at him. So the sun, he start to come down, wanten to meet she there. Sea, he gonna get jealous, putten himself between sand and sun, him come in closer, water coveren up the sand as much as he can and maken sure them never come together. Sun gone, sea go back to his bed. The next day, sun go up again. He looken down at the sand where a bird land, and busy pullen out a piece of weed. He think the sand blowen a kiss, and again he come down, and again the sea come in close. Sun realize is the sea comen between them, maken a plan with clouds to suck him up, spit him down again far away. But the sea, he always finden his own way back again. Sea, he always in-between.

11. WASTED

Truck stop. GIGI and LOLA ready to leave for the day.

GIGI   You got a full can?

LOLA   Very full.

GIGI   Very good. Let me see.

LOLA hands over the can, GIGI unscrews the cap.

Lola, oil, dis, not gasoline.

LOLA   So?

GIGI   Chickn gonna give you ten for oil?

LOLA   Maybe.

GIGI   No. I told you and told you, Lola. Oil not gas. You getten oil you been worken for nothing.

LOLA   Not for nothing, Gigi. Getten oil at least.

GIGI	You got oil, Lola? Where? *(empties can on ground, holding LOLA off)*
LOLA	Don't, Gigi. I been all day getten full.
GIGI	You been all day getten fooled.

GIGI shoves the can into LOLA's hands. LOLA runs off, GIGI goes on to CHICKN's stand.

	Hey.
CHICKN	Hey, where Lola?
GIGI	Lola soon come. *(swinging her heavy can)*
CHICKN	Known you're gonna come back full. My girl, dat. Put down your can and sit by me.
GIGI	I'll sit here. *(elsewhere)*
CHICKN	Now look over there.
GIGI	*(They wait.)* I'm looken.
CHICKN	Remember that yellow shirt Spitty wearen yesterday?
GIGI	Nice shirt, dat. What we looken at?
CHICKN	Spitty gone to the liquor store last week and that girl told him he looken good.
GIGI	That cross–eye girl?

CHICKN	He tell me he don't remember her, but now Spitty gotta put on that one nice yellow shirt every time he want to buy some palm.
GIGI	Ohhh. So what we looken at?
CHICKN	Liquor store closed, and Spitty gone put on that shirt just now.

GIGI looks at CHICKN.

And here they come. Hey Spitty, nice shirt. Your girl, dat? And there they go.

They break up at Spitty's embarrassment. LOLA rushes on, grabs GIGI's can, and tries to unscrew the cap and spill it on the ground with little luck. CHICKN and GIGI move to stop her but CHICKN is faster, shielding LOLA, taking the can.

GIGI	Move, Chickn. She / dead.
CHICKN	Lola!
LOLA	Wasten my whole day.
GIGI	You even too stupid to get mad right. *(flies at her)*
CHICKN	Lola—

He pulls GIGI away from LOLA, then slaps LOLA.

You tired eaten? You tired liven? Go sit down. Don't talk to me. Dis money you spill. Ancestors need money? Spirits need money? Go. Sit.

GIGI	That's it, Chickn. She stayen home from now on. Take her off the road.
CHICKN	Impossible, Gigi. Lola gotta work.
GIGI	Why? Lola don't want this.
CHICKN	You want this? Not a want, work. A need work, this. Gas gotta come in; you gotta bring it, I gotta push it, they gotta burn it.
GIGI	Take her off the road.
CHICKN	Can not, Gigi.
GIGI	Send her back to school.
CHICKN	With what money? School to do what? You're not thinken.
GIGI	Chickn, she got to find some other way.
CHICKN	What other way she got, Gigi? Lola gonna be a doctor? No. Losen enough money already. Lola should have gone to work last spring. Dem was eyen her for a good price already, dem days. Lola wanna eat, then Lola gotta earn. Dis no time for dreamen.
GIGI	Losen money with she on the road now anyways. Chickn, Lola taken oil from Mr. Man today. You gonna make money, that oil? For what, dem few little pennies? She not ready. Dem mens eye'n her for simple. Dem don't care if she eat.
CHICKN	She gonna learn.

GIGI	So hungry you sellen oil now?
CHICKN	You gonna be hungry long before me, Gigi.
GIGI	You gonna let me be hungry?
CHICKN	Never let you.
GIGI	Take her off the road.
CHICKN	You're gonna teach her better, Gigi.
GIGI	She can't learn.
CHICKN	She gotta learn. What gonna happen if she never learn?

They look at LOLA, who is drawing in the dirt with a stick, chastened.

12. TRUCKEN

Truck stop. CHICKN approaches MR. MAN, who is preparing to leave.

CHICKN	You goen past the base?
MR. MAN	First base, yeah. South side.
CHICKN	Needen a ride.
MR. MAN	Gotten lots to carry, eh? Looken like you really need a ride.
CHICKN	Five. *(holds it out)*

MR. MAN	*(takes it)* All right.
CHICKN	Thanks.
MR. MAN	Hold on. That's five for carryen you. Another five, dem cases.
CHICKN	*(deliberates)* Gotten gas, dem cases. Take me to the army base, I given you one can full up, on the other end. Good deal, dat.
MR. MAN	Deal. Get in. *(They begin to drive.)*
CHICKN	Clean truck, dis. You just get inspection?
MR. MAN	Short trip this time. Been three days on the road. Only seven days by the time I come back.
CHICKN	No road for me, man. Liken to keep all my belongings in sight. Gone too long, never known if you're comen back to nothing. How much it's costen you, keepen your house safe when you're gone?
MR. MAN	Dem boys young. Watchen the house for a roof to sleep under. Only spenden money on dem bigger boys to watch the young ones.
CHICKN	Like you worken for free. Same hustle as alla we.
MR. MAN	*(laugh)* No hustle, man. Good money, dis… One of these days, gonna put a wife in that house.
CHICKN	For what? Wife gonna cost you a lot more than all dem boys put together. Even a good wife. Dem well expensive.

MR. MAN	Getten a wife, I'm gonna need more security. Keepen her safe. One of these days.
CHICKN	Sounden like Gigi.
MR. MAN	Who?
CHICKN	Never mind.

MR. MAN drops him off, takes a can, drives away.

One of these days, gonna get a ride further inland. Gonna sell my gas on dem big base, to dem generals. Maken big money.

13. CASSAVA

GIGI's house. Out back for a secret lesson.

GIGI	Come here, Lola. You full up the water and putten them in the pot.
LOLA	*(sings)* Dem girls got dem big ripe cassava.
GIGI	Stupid song.
LOLA	Fat and juicy, make your mouth watah.
	Listen to me, sistah, listen to me, daughtah.
BOTH	Gimme one bite, dem nice, ripe cassava.

GIGI makes a play-biting sound/gesture. LOLA actually bites the cassava in her hand.

GIGI	No, Lola! That's gonna make you plenty sick.·
LOLA	Why dem boys wanten bite cassava if it's gonna make you sick?
GIGI	Which boys?
LOLA	You know, all dem boys at the market, singen that song when we go by. Dem want bite cassava just so. Why dem wanten get sick?
GIGI	Dem boys wanten dead.
LOLA	Can't get dead from any fruit. Fruits only good for eaten. Dem can't kill you.
GIGI	Anything can kill you.
LOLA	Not true, Gigi. Not true. Fruits made for eaten.
GIGI	Water made for drinken, still gonna kill you, if you drown in it. Anything gonna kill you, you use it wrong, Lola.
LOLA	Not anything. Love's not gonna kill you.
GIGI	Even love gonna kill you, you needen it too much. Be all the time careful, Lola.
LOLA	Stop tryen to scare me, Gigi. Gotta be careful. Don't gotta be scared.
GIGI	Don't gotta be, but sometimes it's a good idea. Some things you supposed to 'fraid.

LOLA	(*after a moment*) Sometime I'm gonna make good cassava cake sellen in the market.
GIGI	Yes, and Sometime all your customers dead if you don't do it right. Today too soon for eaten this cassava. What day's today?
LOLA	Thursday.
GIGI	Okay, tell me alla dem again.

LOLA sings the seven steps.

LOLA	Peel cassava Monday. Squeeze cassava Tuesday. Strip cassava Wednesday. Rinse cassava Thursday. (*mumble*) …cassava Friday. Grind cassava Saturday. Fry cassava Sunday. Eat cassava Sunday.
GIGI	What happened Friday?
LOLA	Something very important.
GIGI	Yes, what?
LOLA	You know already, Gigi.
GIGI	Not asken if I know. What you doen Friday?
LOLA	I forget. I got six days right. Forgotten only one.
GIGI	Why we doen seven days?

LOLA shrugs.

Maybe only needen five, we only doen two more for fun. Maybe we don't need dem cassava at all. Let's taken three more days for fun. Let's taken two weeks.

LOLA Can't be taken so long to come ready. Been needen this yesterday. Two weeks gonna be too long.

GIGI So why we been taken seven days?

LOLA shrugs.

Cuz it needs taken seven days. Dry cassava Friday. Dry cassava Friday. You gotta remember alla dem or you're gonna make dem people sick.

LOLA Or dead.

GIGI Or dead. But you're gonna remember, so nobody gonna be dead. Come on, smile. *(singing)* Dem girls got dem big ripe cassava.

LOLA Stupid song.

GIGI Here, dem rinse good now. Gonna drain that water over there *(sends LOLA, begins stoking fire)*, then when the fire is good I'm gonna show you dryen dem. Come bring that stool here.

LOLA Now what?

GIGI Now waiten.

LOLA Tell me something.

GIGI	Not now. I'm busy.
LOLA	Busy with what?
GIGI	Readen. Mailman just come. He bringen this letter from my husband. *(takes out letter)*
LOLA	You got no husband.
GIGI	I know. Mailman comen very early today. Him come deliver me this letter before I get a mailbox. Him deliver this letter before my husband write it, before we married, before him even knowen he gonna love me. That mailman is very, very early.
LOLA	What's in the letter?
GIGI	It's only for me to see. Okay, a little bit.
LOLA	How come he's senden you mail?
GIGI	You want to hear?
LOLA	Yes.
GIGI	Dear Gigi. Pretty Gigi. I longen to come home and see your face. If I can only touchen your face I be so happy. Only wishen I could come home and see you, but I gotta work so I gotta drive. Such a good wife, maken me want to give you anything you need. Getten what you need, taken so much time but I gonna work as hard as I love you; gonna drive as long as I love you. I sending this money for you. Hopen you get plenty food, and have a little extra for a nice dress, too. Love... that's all.

LOLA	Mailman's gonna bring me a very early letter too.
GIGI	Oh yeah?
LOLA	Yeah… Maybe.
GIGI	So, let's see what this letter sayen.
LOLA	Okay. Um. Dear Lola. Um. You so pretty, I am never comen home. Say hello to Gigi and tell her take good care of you. Um. You so pretty. You such a good girl. Love, Mister.

14. EXODUS

CHICKN's stand.

GIGI	*(counts, goes to market)* Chickn, how much you gonna give me, dis?
CHICKN	Ten.
GIGI	No good, Chickn. Gonna be twenty-five today.
CHICKN	What? No way, Gigi. Is how pretty you think you is? Come back tomorrow, I'm gonna give you seven. Costen you three dollars to get your sense back.
GIGI	I don't think so, Chickn. You better gimme twenty-five today. Gonna be costen you thirty tomorrow.
CHICKN	What game you playen, eh? Tryen to starve? You know any these girls gonna give me full for ten.

GIGI	Any which girls? I been watching dis traffic, man. You not been watchen? I been see'n things.
CHICKN	Like what?
GIGI	Last Tuesday, seen ten dem big big trucks come in, ten trucks comen out. Today, is only five trucks come in, twelve trucks comen out. Less gas comen in every day. One day soon dem gas gonna stop, and you wanten to get what's under my bed, not what's in it.
CHICKN	Is true?
GIGI	True. De president pocket leaken, man. Gotten too crowded in there.
CHICKN	Smart, you smart. Knew you was a good girl.
GIGI	Not smart, only gotten my eyes open.
CHICKN	So tell me what else you seen.
GIGI	Seen what's in some of those trucks. A few goen empty. Some gotten yam, wood, and people. People leaven, man. Girls leaven from this road, here. Soon gonna have to go see Mr. Man yourself, you wanten gas. And once dem girls go, you got nothing Mr. Man want...
CHICKN	Smart girl, Gigi. A my girl, dat.
GIGI	A twenty-five dollar, dat.
CHICKN	*(taking her hand)* Dem girls leaven, same ways you been looken, eh?

GIGI	Dem leaven all kinds of ways. Any ways dem can get out, dem goen.
CHICKN	You seen what they see? You goen soon too?
GIGI	You know is not so.
CHICKN	How I know?
GIGI	You know I can't leave. Who's gonna look for my amai? Who's gonna give her water, I'm gone?
CHICKN	But you watchen dem go, hein?
GIGI	Only watchen empty space, dem feet used to stand. Watchen dem prints blown away soon enough. Like dem was never here.

15. PACKEN

GIGI is going through her things. The room is in disarray and a bag sits in the centre.

LOLA	You goen all over again, Gi?
GIGI	Not goen nowhere, Lo.
LOLA	Looken like you're goen.
GIGI	Just bein ready.
LOLA	I wanna be ready too. What we getten ready for?

GIGI	For Sometime, Lo. Thinken I hear footsteps outside the door. Could be him comen soon, and after him come, him go.
LOLA	What should we pack?
GIGI	Don't know. Nobody know what Sometime gonna be like. Better getten ready for anything.
LOLA	Yeah. Anything. Like what?
GIGI	Like... let's packen some condoms in case we needen money when we get there.
LOLA	Oh, then I'm packen dis paper, in case I needen to write a letter to my husband.
GIGI	You packen a pen?
LOLA	For what?
GIGI	I'm packen... pots, for cooken at my new house.
LOLA	I'm packen a towel for the beach.
GIGI	Gotten a beach there, eh?
LOLA	You said. You said we're goen there Sometime. To the beach. You promised.
GIGI	Okay, Lola. We'll go to the beach there. But you got to be ready in case Sometime not easy, too. Understand? In case something go wrong.

LOLA fills a glass with water and sets it in the middle of her bundle.

LOLA	Here. Done.
GIGI	What's that for?
LOLA	In case your new house catch a fire when you cooken.

GIGI puts her arm around LOLA and surveys the room.

16. DUTTY PAPER

GIGI's house. GIGI is outside her door when LOLA enters, wailing, flailing, covered in blood.

GIGI	Lola. Somebody hurt you? Lola, stop crying and tell me. Who done this? Lola, who done this thing?
LOLA	Mr. Man, dat blue truck. Him kill me, Gigi! Him kill me dead! Dead, dis!
GIGI	You not dead yet, Lola. Tell me where it's hurten you.
LOLA	Me dead. Must be me dead, dis much blood and not hurten anywhere. Must be me dead. I'm sorry I haunten you, Gigi. Sorry me get dead. Oh God! Take me to the buryen place now, Gigi, before dem spirits taste my life. Chickn gonna be mad, I haunt him.
GIGI	Not hurten anywhere?

LOLA's wailing.

Where dis blood comen from, Lola?

LOLA wails louder, opens her legs, and begins a warding with dirt and water.

LOLA   Don't leave me here, dis dutty ground, Gigi. Take me to the mopani tree.

GIGI   Hold on. I'm coming right back. You not dead, Lola. You just stupid. Go stand behind the pump. Don't bleed on them roots. Bad juju, dat.

GIGI rummages through a bin and returns with some crumpled newspaper.

Hold out your hand. Do like me, okay?

LOLA unsuccessfully imitates her.

What's that stupid song you been singen?

LOLA   You told me never sing that.

GIGI   Just sing it, nah.

LOLA   Gimme likkle piece o' what you sellen
Gimme one slice dat nice ripe melon
Don't bother wrap that.

GIGI   Okay stop. That's enough.

LOLA   But there's a next part, goes like this...

GIGI   You hear stop?

LOLA   Yes.

GIGI   And what you doing?

LOLA	Stopping now, Gigi.
GIGI	Good. Now do like so.
	Take likkle piece dem paper and roll it Squeeze together knees then sit tight and hold it Dash water 'pon that.
LOLA	*(does it)* How long I'm gonna sit tight like this? It done yet?
GIGI	Gonna be a few days. You stayen home and wait. I'll come see you later.
LOLA	But Chickn—
GIGI	I'll tell him.
LOLA	Mr. Man call me nasty. Say I shoulda known better.
GIGI	I know.
LOLA	I'm not nasty!
GIGI	I know, Lola. Lola, your mother should have told you. Dis gonna happen every month.
LOLA	Every month!
GIGI	Yes.
LOLA	That's nasty.
GIGI	I know.
LOLA	What's a month?

GIGI	It doesn't work if you talk, Lola.
LOLA	Oh.
GIGI	And Lola, you have to take condoms with you from now on. Every time. Every. Time. Hear me?

LOLA adheres to the instruction not to talk.

17. SHAFTED

Truck stop. Music-video lit highway. LOLA and GIGI stand, legs spread, backs to the audience, each holding a gas can. They dance to the music, pumping them old-skool moves; provocative, aggressive, gas vs. ass. GIGI seductively brings the gas can to her lips as the song ends.

GIGI	Hey, Mr. Man. You got too much?
MR. MAN	Yeah. I been looken for somewhere to put it.
GIGI	Big truck, dis. Your truck?
MR. MAN	Not in the truck.
GIGI	You got a room somewhere?
MR. MAN	Over there.
GIGI	Where, dem bushes? No.
MR. MAN	Is when you girls get choosy?
GIGI	No.

MR. MAN	Looken like you don't want this gas.
GIGI	Not a want work. A need work, dis.
MR. MAN	Could be both, hein?
GIGI	Don't. Come in the truck and do your business. I don't need your dutty hands in my hair.
MR. MAN	Come on.

They go to the side. GIGI puts down the gas can as she kneels in front of him.

Close your eyes.

She does. He takes the can and puts it to her lips.

Know what this is?

GIGI nods. He holds her throat and suddenly tips the can back. There is not much in it, but GIGI gags. He pushes her into the bushes.

You want it? I know you do. Show me how much you want this.

GIGI	Don't.
MR. MAN	Slow.

LOLA moves to the reprise, leaving with someone as it ends, as GIGI re-enters from bushes.

(*pushing her out*) Go on.

GIGI	You gonna fill me up now.
MR. MAN	I don't think so, honey.
GIGI	You gonna fill me up!
MR. MAN	You plenty full up already.
GIGI	This my work. Ain't no Chucky, me. You gotta fill me up!
MR. MAN	Get out of here. Go. GO. *(walks away casually)*
GIGI	Gonna fix you, Mr. Man. I find you, I gonna hurt you. I get sick, I gonna curse you. I die, I gonna haunt you.

> *MR. MAN starts the truck and leaves. The truck, too, sounds unaffected. LOLA enters, swinging a half-full can.*

LOLA	Let's go see Chickn.
GIGI	Mm.
LOLA	Gigi, where your can?
GIGI	Don't have it.
LOLA	No can?
GIGI	No.
LOLA	Then whatchu doing with Mr. Man?
GIGI	Nothing. Lola, go away.

LOLA	Tell me about de president pocket… Something on your back, G… Wait, slow down. Let me get it… Did you fall?
GIGI	Get lost, Lola.

LOLA does, kicking dirt by the roadside.

LOLA	I am. I'm gonna get lost Sometime. Sometime gonna go cross the border and gone. I know the way. Seen them fat men coming over this way. Only gotta go back the same way, goen where the gas come from. That side, gonna be comen easy. Gas gonna flow. Good days gonna come. You gonna come find me, gonna tell me come back home. Only talken me softly. Only touchen me gently.
GIGI	*(returning)* Lola. Come on. Don't stay here. *(leaving)*
LOLA	Okay. Gi, I remembered. You said we gotta be clean, always.
GIGI	*(They walk a short way, before she reconsiders.)* No, go follow Chickn.
LOLA	But—
GIGI	Get lost. Go.

LOLA leaves. GIGI goes home and counts out her money. Not enough. Thinks.

Chickn.

Love for gas
Gas for cash

Cash for living
Living for love.

18. THIS LITTLE PIGGY WENT TO MARKET

The road—between. GIGI is fuming and calculating, walking over toward the market where LOLA is speaking quietly to CHICKN. He sees GIGI coming.

GIGI   Hey, man. Needen something.

CHICKN   You nothing but need. How I'm gonna take you on? You seen me worken. Seen me sweaten. You ever seen me when you need nothing? Never. You think another man like me gonna come so easy? Think I don't know you girls? Plenty smart men marry with dem eyes closed. Think dem go to bed with good girls, but is Chucky dem wake next to. After that, is lucky if dem ever wake up again. My eyes open, Gigi. Mi nah want fi dead.

GIGI   *(rushing to him)* Chickn, listen, I—

CHICKN   It's okay, Gigi. Lola gonna stay here today.

GIGI   Chickn, I gotta talk to you.

CHICKN   Yeah, maybe another time.

GIGI   Chickn, you need to help me.

CHICKN   What you done for me? Huh, Gigi? Seem like you killen time, waiten on some good chance.

GIGI   Not waiten anything, Chickn.

CHICKN	Why you never wanna go to the beach?
GIGI	What?
CHICKN	I'm wondering where you been when I'm gone to the beach, when I'm gone to the base, when I don't have you under my eye. You been lonely?
GIGI	You know where. Lola was with me.
LOLA	You told me to get lost.
GIGI	Shut up, Lola.
CHICKN	You don't want her to talk, or you don't want me to hear?
GIGI	Listen, Chickn. / That man, he hurt me.
CHICKN	*(schupzing)* / I must look like a fool.
GIGI	Did you hear me?
CHICKN	I hear something.
GIGI	What you hear?
CHICKN	What you done?
GIGI	What you hear?
CHICKN	I hear you sellen empty cans now, Gigi. Seen you comen back swingen your hands. Where your can gone? Thought you was working. Do so good, you only walking the road for good times?
GIGI	Chickn, you gonna help me?

CHICKN	I gonna help you. You gonna help me, yeah? *(lewd gesture)*
GIGI	…yeah… okay *(moves toward him)*
CHICKN	*(cringing)* I don't want that. I can't get no sick, Gigi.
GIGI	Lola—
CHICKN	Lola doing fine. She don't need your ways.
GIGI	Chickn—
CHICKN	Chucky, you. *(throws a rock close to her)*
LOLA	Chucky, you. *(giggles)*

19. FUMING

GIGI's house. GIGI returns home. Counts money again, carefully, willing it to be more. Goes to the gas storage area, fuming. Pulls out two cans of differing sizes and glares, thinks, presses each nozzle against the heel of her palm, closes her eyes, and presses them to the back of her neck, puts them back. Pulls one out again. Distortion of previous dance. Pensive rage. Smolder. Blaze. Smolder.

20. FIXED

Truck stop. GIGI is skulking in the shadows. MR. MAN pulls over and stands by the roadside to take a piss in the grass. GIGI puts gas can nozzle against the back of his neck. He stiffens.

GIGI	Know what this is?
MR. MAN	Yes.
GIGI	Do you want it?

She hands him another gas can.

You owe me a can, Mr. Man. Now, we going over to that truck and you gonna fill me up. Don't slow.

LOLA	Gigi! Gigi! Want a chocolate?
GIGI	Go away from here, Lola.
LOLA	*(giggling)* Gigi, you oiling Mr. Man's neck? He squeaky?
GIGI	Lola—

MR. MAN strikes GIGI, who falls, dropping the gas can. LOLA rushes to save the gas. MR. MAN takes her hand.

MR. MAN	You want it?

LOLA nods.

Lemme see.

She covers a finger in gas and puts it in her mouth, sucking on it.

Come on.

LOLA follows him out with both cans. When they are gone, GIGI gets up, removes her shirt, mops up gas, then goes toward the bushes where they have disappeared.

LOLA	Gigi say no cutten. No cutten, Gigi say
GIGI	Move, Lola.

She lights the shirt to throw it in the b̶̶̶̶ ̶̶ goes up in a blaze in her hands. She falls and is kicked violently by MR. MAN, who runs to his truck, dropping his wallet in the process. LOLA picks up the wallet and nudges GIGI curiously before leaving.

21. SOMETIME COME

CHICKN's stand. CHICKN and LOLA sitting at the market. LOLA is trying to lean her head on CHICKN's shoulder. CHICKN is trying to count money.

CHICKN	This your day off, Lola? You join a union? Go on.
LOLA	Where should I go?
CHICKN	Where did you go yesterday?
LOLA	The truck stop.
CHICKN	How about the day before?
LOLA	The truck stop.
CHICKN	Lola, you gonna ask me every day where to go?
LOLA	I do it wrong you gonna get mad.
CHICKN	*(loses count)* Lola! Lola, go.

LOLA	Where should I go?
CHICKN	Follow Mimi, okay?
LOLA	Don't wanna go with Mimi. Mimi always taken my man. Gigi say, "No kissing. No cutting. No cuddling up. No freebies. No taken my man."
CHICKN	*(looks at her)* That's good. Gigi teach you good.
LOLA	When Gigi comen back?
CHICKN	Sometime.
LOLA	Oh. Chickn, when Sometime comen?
CHICKN	Never.
LOLA	Oh. Chickn, when Never comen?
CHICKN	Forget it.
LOLA	Okay. Chickn, wanna hold my hand?
CHICKN	Get outta here, Lola.
LOLA	Chickn.
CHICKN	WHAT?
LOLA	*(handing him the wallet)* Found this under Mr. Man's truck after he run away. Told Gigi, but she was sleepen.
CHICKN	Why didn't you tell me before? *(taking and counting the contents)*

LOLA	I forgot.
CHICKN	Next time remember, okay? *(putting his arm around her)* Good girl.

22. NEW MATH

Truck stop / truck's cab. CHICKN and MR. MAN strike a deal. CHICKN is counting money as MR. MAN and LOLA drive away together. LOLA's ribbon is tied to his rear-view mirror.

MR. MAN	Talk. Say something, girl.
LOLA	How far you goen today?
MR. MAN	Same far as you.
LOLA	Oh. Sorry. *(silence)*
MR. MAN	You want some chocolate? *(She nods, takes it.)* Talk to me.
LOLA	Talk about what?
MR. MAN	Anything. Only wanten to hear you. Tell me any little nonsense in your head.
LOLA	But Gigi said—
MR. MAN	Who's Gigi?
LOLA	Nobody.

MR. MAN	So tell me. Anything.
LOLA	Well, Mr. Man—
MR. MAN	My name is Henry, girl. You gonna call me Henry now.
LOLA	Henry. *(giggle)* Dem time before, I used to be standen by the road there. Trucks go by fast, dust flyen up over me and I'm closen my eyes and thinken how all dem dust was something else before it came over me. All dem dust come from under people's foot, from off people tires, and from on the wind blowen in every direction. So even though I'm standen still dis one truck stop, I'm touchen all these other placs. This one dust in my eye off a tire, dat truck comen from near the ocean, on the other side, maybe that dust float on the ocean from farland where we will never see, but I'm touchen it. This dust in my nose, maybe used to be down in the ground holden a mopani root down tightly so dem ancients can stay where dey is. This dirt on my tongue come off the skin of one strong hunter chasing his meat on the sands way up north. So I'm thinken, I been all over and I always been happy to see dem trucks go by, because I know dem trucks bringen the whole world here. I always been happy. Henry. Henry. Henry?
MR. MAN	Yes?
LOLA	Dis Sometime?
MR. MAN	Sure.

LOLA pulls a glass of water from her bag and drinks it.

GIGI   Love for gas
             Gas for cash
             Cash for living
             Living for love.

                  Fin.

ACKNOWLEDGEMENTS

My thanks to the workshop actors—Kevin Jones, Cara Ricketts, and Jamal Grant—for their questions and their clarity; my thanks to the members of the New Harlem advisory committee and to producer Yvette Nolan for both pushing this forward and holding me up. Thanks to Philip Adams, Kern Albert, Nir Bareket, and Jody Hanson for their contributions to research.

The writing and development of this play was financially supported by project funding from the Ontario Arts Council, the Canada Council for the Arts, and the Toronto Arts Council, including support through the Ontario Arts Council's Theatre Creators' Reserve Program via recommender bcurrent. Additional contributions toward development were made through the Enbridge playRites Award, the Queen's University Drama Department, Thousand Islands Playhouse, Theatre Passe Muraille's BUZZ Festival, and the sustained support of Native Earth Performing Arts.

Donna-Michelle St. Bernard is a prolific wordsling-er, working for change through the arts as an emcee, playwright, and administrator. Notable works for the stage include *Salome's Clothes*, *The First Stone*, and *Cake*. She has been playwright-in-residence at Obsidian Theatre, lead vocalist for Belladonna & the Awakening, and contributor to Afrotoronto. com. DM is currently the general manager of Native Earth Performing Arts and artistic director of New Harlem Productions.